Prayer for the Beatification of Francis Tregian

Lord, we come before you with joy in our hearts. We believe that you bestowed upon your servant, Francis Tregian, the gift of an outstanding love for you in the Holy Mass. Through his suffering he gave heroic witness to the ministry of Peter for the unity of the Church.

Grant that we may love you as he did, and be as steadfast in the practice of our Faith. For our encouragement, and in recognition of his extraordinary devotion, we ask you to confer on him the honours of the altar.

We ask this through Christ our Lord. Amen.

With Ecclesiastical approval
✠ CHRISTOPHER
Plymouth. 7th August, 199(

FRANCIS TREGIAN
1548–1608
Elizabethan recusant

A TRULY CATHOLIC CORNISHMAN

Raymond Francis Trudgian

THE *Alpha* PRESS

BRIGHTON • PORTLAND

2 4 6 8 10 9 7 5 3 1

First published 1998 in Great Britain by
THE ALPHA PRESS
Box 2950
Brighton BN2 5SP

and in the United States of America by
THE ALPHA PRESS
5804 N.E. Hassalo St.
Portland, Oregon 97213-3644

British Library Cataloguing in Publication Data

A CIP catalogue record for this book is available from the British Library.

Printed by Selwood Printing Ltd., Burgess Hill.
This book is printed on acid-free paper

CONTENTS

LISBON PULPIT MESSAGE 1

SO MUCH TO LOSE 4

RELIGIOUS FERMENT 6

A PRIEST AT GOLDEN 10

CORPUS CHRISTI CONFRONTATION 13

THE MARTYRDOM OF ST CUTHBERT MAYNE 15

TREGIAN'S TRIALS 19

GOLDEN IS TAKEN 24

PRISON POETRY 26

FAREWELL TO CORNWALL 28

THE FLEET 30

CATHOLIC SETBACKS 32

INTO EXILE 34

A MIRROR FOR US ALL 36

TREGIAN'S DESCENDANTS 41

SOURCES USED 45

VISITS 46

ACKNOWLEDGEMENTS 47

ABOUT THE AUTHOR 48

INDEX 49

LISBON PULPIT MESSAGE

The rains had come at last and a group of Lisbon college students and their tutor took the funicular railway that runs up to the square and the impressive church of St. Roque. They had come to see the Church and museum, which had been closely associated with the establishment of the Society of Jesus in Portugal. The church had provided a springboard for their significant missionary role in India and Japan. St Francis Xavier had preached here in 1541, before setting sail for Goa at the invitation of King John III to evangelize the East Indies. He was fortified by a papal brief nominating him apostolic nuncio in the East.

The students stood before the impressive pink marble pulpit imagining the missionary fervour of that sermon preached long ago. The tutor, however, directed their thoughts to a strange inscription chipped out by some English Catholics in the centre of the pulpit. After struggling with the stilted Portugese and the style of the carving they found themselves reading about another Francis:

Here stands the body of DOM FRANCISCO TREGIAN,
an illustrious English gentleman.
After his estates were confiscated and he had endured 28 years' imprisonment for the Catholic Faith during the reign of Queen Elizabeth,
died in the City of Lisbon with great fame and saintliness in the year 1608, 25 September. Seventeen years after he was buried in the church of St. Roque belonging to the Society of Jesus, on the 25th April 1625 his body was found entire and incorrupt,and here deposited in this pulpit by English Catholics
who were resident in this City on 25th April 1626

The questions from the students came thick and fast. *Where were his estates? How did he end up in Lisbon? Where was his first tomb? Why*

PULPIT INSCRIPTION
S. ROQUE CHURCH, LISBON

AQUI ESTA EM PE O CORPO DE DOM
Here stands the body of DOM
FRANCISCO TREGIAN FIDALGO IN-
FRANCIS TREGIAN English gentleman
GRES MUI ILLUSTRE: E QUAL DEPOIS
and illustrious: who after
DE COFISCADOS SEVS ESTADOS E
the confiscation of his estates and
GRANDES TRABALHOS PADECI-
great sufferings endured
DOS EM.28. ANNOS DE PRISAM POLLA
in the 28 years imprisonment for
DEFESA DA FE CATOLICA EM INGR-
the defence of the Catholic faith during
RA PERSEGVCAM DA RAINHA ISA-
the persecution in the reign of Eliza-
BEL NO ANNO DE 1608. A 25 DEZ
beth in the year 1608 25th Dec [actual month Sept]
MORREO NESTA CIDADE DE LISBOA
died in the city of Lisbon
COM GRANDE FAMA DE SANTIDA
with great fame and saintliness.
DE AVENDO. 17.ANNOS 2 ESTAVA
17 years after he was buried
SEPULTADO NESTA IGREIIA DE
in the tomb in the church of
S. ROQUE DA COMP DE HIS NO
St. Rock belonging to the Society of Jesus
DE 1625. AOS. 25 ABRIL SE A
in 1625, on 25th April
CHOV SEV CORPO INTEIRO E-
his body was found entire and
INCORRUPTO E FOI COLLOCADO
incorrupt and was here deposited
NESTE LVGAR PELLOS INGRESES
in this pulpit by English
CATOLICOS RESIDENTES NESTA
Catholics resident in this
CICADE AOS 25 DE ABRIL DE 1626
city on 25th April 1626.

was he buried standing up? Why did a person renowned for his saintliness spend almost half his life in prison? The answers reveal a fascinating story about a man who has been confined to a footnote in history. He is either mentioned as the patron of the first seminary priest to be martyred under Elizabeth, St Cuthbert Mayne, or as the father of the younger Francis who was to collect together the music of William Byrd and other important composers into what is now known as the Fitzwilliam Virginal.

Francis Tregian is buried "standing up" to remind us that he stood up to Queen Elizabeth and her Act of Supremacy, making her Supreme Governor of the Church, and the Act of Uniformity which forced everyone to conform to the new church and forms of worship. Those who refused to attend worship "as by law established" were called "Recusants". Francis was the first to lose all his lands and possessions, and spent almost thirty years in prison for refusing to attend the new service and for sheltering a Catholic priest. For him the true faith was the Catholic Faith established not by law but by grace, when Pope Gregory sent St Augustine to the shores of England in 597 AD.

Francis could have succumbed and spent his days with his family, riding over his vast estates in Cornwall which stretched from shore to shore, the wind blowing in his hair. Every day, he could have watched the sun rise over the English Channel and set over the Atlantic Ocean. Instead he spent half his life in damp, filthy conditions in prison in London and was to die in Lisbon in exile. He was proud to be labelled "recusant" because by his refusal to conform and face loss of lands and imprisonment he sought to witness to the basic human right of freedom of worship and freedom of conscience. His story is an inspiration, especially to lay people, as Francis himself was, to hold on to the faith, whatever the circumstances.

The origin of the Tregian family is shrouded in mystery. Pronounced "Trudgian" it is spelt in a variety of ways in Elizabethan documents. Some argue for a Breton origin, with the suggestion that the family came over with William in 1066. A strong oral tradition links them with the Phoenicians who came to Cornwall trading in tin, and who settled there.

We know for certain that the family wealth was built up in the tin-mining industry around St Ives. A series of astute marriages took them "*loftily above the flight of Cornish gentry*" into royal connections and service at Court, which is where we first find Francis at the age of twenty-four in 1572.

The family had by then moved to central Cornwall becoming tin merchants and shipowners. The first marriage recorded is in 1349, of John Tregian to Joanne, daughter of Stephen Trewarthenick of Tregony, head of the influential Boscowan family.

In 1456 Thomas Tregian, an attorney as well as shipowner, was given a licence to take pilgrims on his ship "*Mary*" to what was then the important shrine of the apostle St James the Great at Santiago de Compostela just south of La Coruna. In turn his son Thomas, a leading merchant in Truro, was to use his ship "*Jesus*" for the same purpose. This involvement with Spain is important for an understanding of the family and the subsequent events in the life of Francis. By 1512 the young Thomas had bought up several manors including Tregian Manor at St. Ewe.

His son John was to increase the family property by marrying Jane, of the ancient and wealthy Wolvedon family of Probus. It brought into the family the Manor home of "Golden" – a corruption of Wolvedon. He set to work to make this old house into an appropriate family residence. The records state it was "*a manor place richly begun and amply, but not ended, called Wolvedon – alias Golden*". As well as being granted a life monopoly of exporting cowhides out of Cornwall, he was Esquire to the Body of Henry VIII and Steward of the Chamber. His daughter Elizabeth was to marry Sir Richard Edgcumbe, and the Tregians becoming even more interwoven with West Country nobility.

The marriage, which very much affects our story, was the marriage of John, son and heir to John of Golden. He married Katherine daughter of Sir John and Lady Elizabeth Arundell of Laherne near St. Mawgan. His mother was Eleanor, daughter of Thomas Grey, who was half brother to Elizabeth of York, wife of Henry VII, mother of Henry VIII and therefore ironically the grandmother of Elizabeth I who was to be the scourge of the family.

The son of this powerful union is the subject of our story, Francis Tregian. He married Mary, eldest daughter of Charles, seventh Lord Stourton, who was Lady Arundell's first husband. At their marriage both Francis and Mary were connected to the highest in the land at the centre of a wealthy cultural circle. The circle was described as "lovers of music with scholarly tastes", with the Catholic Church at the heart of its life.

Such concentrated wealth and influence was to breed envy from other families especially the Grenvilles, and in particular Richard, whose smouldering hatred of the young Francis was to burst into flames and engulf them all. His father had tried to marry his daughter Margaret to John, Francis' father, but was passed over for an Arundell. Representing the seafaring, anti-Spanish, anti-Pope families, Richard had already fallen foul of the land-owning Sir John Arundell and Francis who served on a commission on piracy, which was very prevalent around the Cornish shores.

RELIGIOUS FERMENT

The Catholics in Cornwall had already been aroused by an earlier Act of Uniformity in 1549. From June 9 of that year all had to conform to the first Book of Common Prayer with its services in English. This was to replace the Mass which they had known for centuries and in which their childhood had been cradled.

The Cornish staged their famous "Prayer Book Rebellion" calling the new liturgy a "Christmas game". They confronted Thomas Cranmer with the statement that as they were Cornish speaking they knew no English. Not knowing the scholastic nature of the Catholics in Cornwall, Cranmer asked them sarcastically if they knew any Latin either.

There was no doubt that the Catholic Church itself was in need of reform. In 1568 Pope St Pius V had reformed the Breviary making it clearer and simpler, restoring the Psalms and the reading of the Bible to their dominant place. This was according to the decrees of the Council of Trent. The copy the Pope used can be seen in the church of St Mary Maggiore in Rome and "*it became in his hands the hoe by which he uprooted a whole world of weeds*".

At the age of 24, the young Francis returned from the Continent with a fervour to spread the renewed Catholic faith to the influential nobles at the court of Queen Elizabeth. His name is first officially listed under the Queen's Act of 1571, which threatened loss of goods and lands for life if the individual left the country without licence and failed to return within six months. Already married and living at Golden Manor, Francis returned in the next year and is listed with twenty others in 1572 who were described as "*fugitives from abroad*".

It is typical of Francis that his zeal, combined with stubbornness, should lead him to proclaim the Catholic Faith in the strongly anti-Catholic atmosphere of the Court. His grandfather, John, had served under Henry VIII and Francis was "reverting to type", enjoying the glamour and excitement and even the danger of preaching the faith under the very noses of those who were trying to extinguish it forever.

Ironically, with his aristocratic background and connections he became the perfect courtier, possessing that rare quality, integrity, in all that he did. He even went out from the Court into the poverty-stricken districts of London, "*increasing religious fervour in the hearts of the depressed*" at the same time winning their friendship and gratitude.

So favoured was he at first that the Queen offered to make Francis a Viscount. Francis turned it down with a typical reply, "*To me it would be quite enough if the Faith, for the sake of which I came to Court, should breathe more freely and recover strength.*" The Queen was not well pleased with this reply and the next thing we hear is of Francis returning to Golden in rather a hurry.

A grandson of Francis through his daughter Philippa, Father Francis Plunkett of the Order of St. Benedict, says his hurried exit from Court was because of his refusal to respond to the amorous advances of the Queen. There is no other evidence for this and Plunkett's comment could be seen as the response of a family, much maligned and dispossessed, trying to get their revenge on the Queen. One thing which does ring true about the incident, however, is that he did not actually refuse to come to her bedchamber but instead sent a message to say that he was unwell!

A far more likely reason was that his proselytising zeal had become too dangerous. The danger came from the head-to-head conflict between the Pope and the Queen as they sought the religious allegiance of the people of England. In 1570 Pope St Pius V, thinking it would give support to a Catholic revolt in the North, issued the Bull, *Regnans in Excelsis*, which excommunicated and deposed the Queen, declared that she and all her adherents were no part of the Body of Christ, and released all subjects from allegiance to her. This was to have the effect of all Catholics being treated as traitors. The response of the English Parliament was swift and

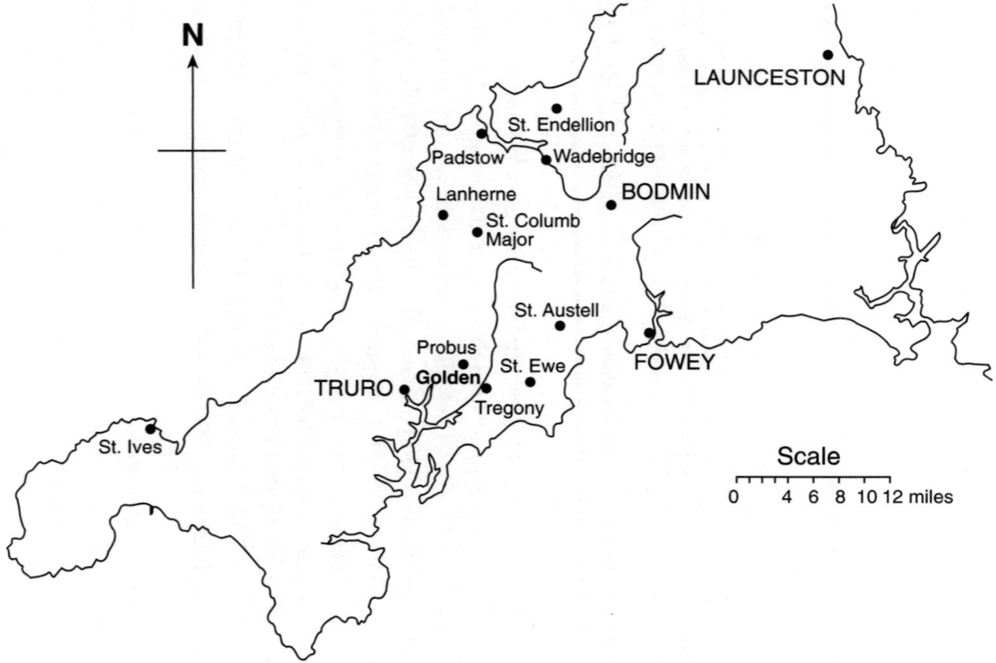

Sketch map of 16th century Cornwall

severe, the Act of 1571 subjecting to the penalty of treason anyone who reconciled another to Rome or was himself reconciled to Rome.

Those who refused to attend the new services, the "recusants", were to be heavily fined. Some Catholics compromised and for form's sake, and to escape the fine, attended the services but just observed from the back or even wandered around, heckling. Even priests were known to follow outwardly one religion and believe another. One notorious turncoat was a Dr Perne, Master of Peterhouse College, Cambridge. He changed his allegiance several times and was taken aback when a sincere laywoman asked him to tell her honestly and simply which was the holy religion that would see her safe to heaven. Unused to such a direct questioning, the Doctor eventually replied "*If you wish, you can live in the religion which the Queen and the whole nation profess – you will have a good life and have none of the vexations which the Catholics have to suffer. But don't die in it. Die in faith and communion with the Catholic Church, that is, if you want to save your soul.*" Sadly for him, in the light of his reply, he died not long afterwards at Lambeth Palace, after dining with the Archbishop of Canterbury!

For Francis there could never be any compromise, his Catholic Faith pervaded the whole of his life and was to be the faith by which he would die. The religious ferment made him even more determined to support and strengthen his fellow Catholics in Cornwall. The only way to do that was to provide the Mass for the faithful on a regular basis. That would mean finding a priest with the faith and courage to come and live at Golden to carry out what had become an illegal and treasonable ceremony.

A PRIEST AT GOLDEN

There were those, like the Lancashire-born priest William Allen, who felt that because of the increasing difficulties of promoting the Catholic Faith in England the only answer was to go into exile on the Continent. Educated at Oriel College, Oxford he founded the English College at Douai on 19 September 1568. Based on the Oxford model, it was to prepare Catholic scholars for the day when England would return to the Catholic Faith.

However, the situation was deteriorating so rapidly it was decided that there was an urgent necessity for clergy to prepare for *immediate* work in England to provide the Mass and support the faithful Catholics who were holding on to their religion despite all the odds. The English Government called persons so ordained on the Continent *seminary priests*, that is, a priest ordained outside the Queen's dominions by the See of Rome and thereby stamped as a traitor.

A Devonian, Cuthbert Mayne, was among the first of these priests to be trained and ordained and sent to England. This mild, academic and saintly West-country man seemed an unlikely person to be at the centre of the violent and bloody drama which was to unfold at Golden.

Cuthbert had been previously ordained into the new Anglican Church and only returned to the "old religion" after much soul-searching at Oxford. Born on St Cuthbert's Day, 1543, at Youlston, North Devon of humble farming stock, he was educated at Barnstable Grammar School. His uncle, an Anglican priest "got him made a minister" and he was given the living of Huntshaw parish at the age of 17! He later stated that "*he knew nothing at that time what religion or ministry meant*". He went on to St Albans Hall, Oxford (now Merton College) and became chaplain to St Johns College. He took his MA in 1570 and by that time had come under the influence of Gregory Martin, who was to be instrumental in translating the

Douai version of the Bible, and the famous Edmund Campion. When they left Oxford, correspondence between them fell into the hands of the Bishop of London, who ordered Cuthbert's arrest at Oxford. A fellow Devonian friend at Oxford, Thomas Ford, gave him a warning and Cuthbert fled to the West Country, again wrestling with the decision he had to make, knowing the heartache it would bring to his family. It is thought that he stayed with his friends the Arundells of Laherne and left for Douai through the nearby port of Padstow on the north Cornish coast. The Channel port of Fowey would have been closely watched.

Cuthbert Mayne was ordained in1575, gained his Bachelor of Theology degree in 1576, and immediately set sail for England with fellow priest John Paine, who was to be martyred in 1582. It appears that, like many travellers, Mayne did some shopping before he left and he was to lose his luggage on the journey. Both of these factors were to play a part in his eventual capture and death the following year.

From a bookseller in Douai he purchased a printed copy of the Papal Bull for the Jubilee Year 1575. He certainly could not have bought it in Rome as was to be alleged. Pope Gregory XIII had given a licence for it to be printed in the diocese. He must have bought it as a souvenir because it was already out of date. It took the form of Jubilee indulgence by which plenary forgiveness of sins could be obtained by visits to certain basilicas in Rome by the faithful, and an extension to those, such as in England, who could not make the journey.

The second item he bought was a waxen Agnus-Dei, the sign of the Lamb of God, made from an Easter candle blessed by the Pope in St Peters. This was to count against him at his trial. After being delayed for some time by stormy seas, Mayne and Paine discovered that their luggage had fallen into the hands of government officers watching the ports. This "lost" luggage was returned through the good services of an Englishman, Richard Evingham, but it is thought that the contents of theological books, notes and "objects of piety" were carefully noted. And both were marked men as they went their separate ways. Cuthbert made his way to the home of "certain of his friends". Even on the last day of his life he refused to give their names but it is thought they were the Arundells who had a house in Clerkenwell, London. It is they who directed him to the Tregian family of Golden Manor.The young Francis was delighted to welcome Cuthbert because it meant that the many Catholics on his estates could now have the Mass celebrated for them. Mayne, wearing the clothes and bearing of a Steward, was able to move freely over much of central Cornwall strengthening the Catholics in their faith, teaching, preaching and administering the much longed for Mass. The secret venues for this service were marked by placing sheets on the hedges at crossroads. The sighting of "snow on the hedges" meant that the Mass was being celebrated that day.

CORPUS CHRISTI CONFRONTATION

The feast of Corpus Christi is a day of special thanksgiving for the Mass. In 1577 it fell on June 8 and was to be a day of double celebration as the Catholic families gathered at Golden to give thanks for a year of Cuthbert Mayne's pastoral and sacramental care.

Instead, remote Golden Manor became the flash point of the frustrations and tensions which had built up at national and international level in both religion and politics.

For whatever reason, Queen Elizabeth was determined to make Francis pay for his early exit from Court. As he was a Catholic with extensive and wealthy estates she summoned her cousin, Sir George Carey, the Knight Marshal, instructing him to proceed against Tregian with the utmost rigour and without delay. The reward was to be the Tregian estates which would fall to Carey under the law of *praemunire* which made it an offence against the Crown to assert that the Pope had supremacy in England. Sir George Carey immediately got in touch with the arch-enemy of Francis, Richard Grenville, who had been made Sheriff of Cornwall in 1576 with supreme powers throughout the County. He needed no further excuse. The episode of Mayne's "lost luggage" supports the theory that the authorities were already monitoring the events at Golden.

The new Anglican religion was not going well in the West Country. An obstinate spirit of resistance remained after the Prayer Book rebellion. William Bainbridge, the aged Protestant Bishop of Exeter, was urged by the Lords of Council to act with more severity. Perhaps it is no coincidence that in June 1577 he was in nearby Truro trying to win the recusants over to the new religion. At the age of seventy-five, of a peaceful and retiring nature, his heart was not in it, "*he could not prevail with the recusants or work them to any good conformity*". When the young, energetic and ambitious Grenville met him in Truro and alerted him to the Tregian affair, he was only too glad to lend his support to the proposed action and let the secular arm take over.

The trumped-up reason for surrounding Golden on 8 June was that as Sheriff, Grenville was looking for a fugitive named Anthony Bourne, an escaped prisoner. This was despite the fact that the Sheriffs of other counties had given up the search knowing that Bourne had left the country in March!

When Grenville appeared on the doorstep of Golden with "eight or nine JPs" and over a hundred armed men, he demanded that he search the house for Bourne. Francis denied all knowledge of the man and demanded to see the Queen's warrant.

Grenville then drew his dagger and forced his way in. Obviously no Bourne was to be found but they came to a locked door. At this moment Cuthbert Mayne was in the garden, but hearing the commotion, came into his room from the outside and opened the door just as it was being beaten down. Grasping him by the collar Grenville cried out, "*What art thou?*" "*A man*", Cuthbert replied. This further incensed Grenville who ripped open his doublet looking for a coat of mail. Instead he found an even greater prize, the waxen Agnus-Dei, a forbidden object under Elizabethan law.

Mayne's papers books and letters, including one from Gregory Martin, and the Papal Bull were rushed with Cuthbert himself to Bishop Brainbridge, waiting in Truro.

Richard Grenville had reaped a harvest beyond his wildest dreams. As possession of a Papal Bull meant death he knew he had enough to hang the priest and to ruin his master Tregian for life. As a bonus thirty-one other Catholic recusants were arrested from the leading Catholic families of Cornwall, including the Arundells.

THE MARTYRDOM OF ST CUTHBERT MAYNE

Francis Tregian was allowed to return home from Truro on a surety of £2000. Because of their importance both he and Sir John Arundell were to be sent to London for trial before the Council. The others, including the historian Nicholas Roscarrock, who was to meet up with Arundell in the Tower and Tregian in the Fleet prison, were taken to Launceston for trial.

Cuthbert Mayne was personally, and humiliatingly, paraded by Richard Grenville through the villages of Cornwall to Launceston Castle. There, huge iron weights were placed on his legs and he was thrown into the most dreadful dungeon to await his trial in three months' time.

In mid-September 1577 he was tried with sixteen others, all friends and servants of the Tregian family. The prosecutor was Sir John Popham, later to become Attorney General. The Judges were Sir Roger Manwood and Sir John Jeffreys.

Briefly, the six accusations against the priest, in which he was aided and abetted by the others, were as follows:

1. On the first day of October 1576 he obtained a Bull from Rome.
2. He had published the same Bull at Golden.
3. On February 14, 1576, he had extolled and promulgated the authority of the Pope.
4. That he had brought into the county an Agnus-Dei blessed by the Pope himself and gave it to Francis Tregian.
5. In September 1576 he did deliver eleven of these Agnus-Deis to other persons
6. That on 1 June (8th?) 1577 did publicly celebrate Mass in the Popish fashion. (The indictment reads "*For the saying of Mass: Cuthbert Mayne, Auctor: Francis Tregian, Procuror*".)

The shopping trip in Douai, as we mentioned before, was to have fatal consequences. Although Judge Jeffreys and some of the jury were persuaded that Mayne had never been to Rome and that the Jubilee Bull now had no force, Grenville harangued the jury until they came up with a unanimous verdict of guilty. Manwood, the senior Judge, angrily overruled Jeffreys, describing Mayne as "*a Romisher and a hidden traitor to the realm of the Queen*".

The evidence for conducting the Mass was also circumstantial. It stated that Grenville had found in Mayne's room "an iron instrument with which he fashioned his god (irons for making altar bread) together with a towel for wiping chalices and a Missal". The following day, when sentence was given, Manwood again overruled Jeffreys and the death sentence for traitors was given: "*Mayne was to be drawn to a place to be hung until half dead. Then should his privy parts and entrails be ripped out and burnt in thy sight.*"

Mayne had already denied he was a traitor by expressing his love for his country. On hearing the sentence he lifted up his eyes and hands with the prayer "*Deo gratias*". As said those words of thanks to God all observed the *gentle happiness of his countenance.* Cuthbert was to remain in his foul cell for three more months, heavily fettered.

The delay was caused by the Privy Council being uneasy about his case, especially as Judge Jeffreys had raised an objection to the death penalty. A meeting was summoned for all the judges of the realm. Despite being divided they eventually decided that Mayne should be executed on November 30, the Feast of St Andrew, as a terror to the Papists".

Richard Grenville had rushed to London to get a warrant for the execution, although strangely, it was to be the Deputy Sheriff, his cousin George Grenville, who was to supervise the dreadful act.

On 28th November Mayne was told that he was to die in three days time. He prepared himself in prayer and meditation. It was said on that night a great light shone from his cell.

On the 29th from 8.00 a.m. until dusk he was forced to stand in irons, with his hands manacled, to answer questions put by "gentlemen and two ministers of the reformed religion". The Public Records contain this examination in full. The nine statements are signed by Cuthbert Mayne's own hand, "*These things affirmed by me Cuthbert Mayne I think to be trewe*".

He was forced to admit that he came from beyond the seas to the West Country to work for Tregian, but would not name the friends who obtained the post, neither would he say where and when he celebrated the Mass. His only contact with Sir John Arundell had been with his Master, Tregian, or at the behest of his Master.

He was asked what his position would be if the Pope or any other by his authority made war against the Queen. Although he loved his country he declared that the establishment of the faith came first, the *Queen neither ever was, nor is, nor ever shall be, head of the Church in England.* He also supported the rights of the recusants to refuse to attend, or even hear, the new "*Schismaticall service*".

Finally, he showed his compassion, asking for favour for his own man, John Hodges, one of Tregian's men, stating that he was "*not privy to any of the doings in Religion*". On Market day, 30th November 1577,the execution was carried out in Launceston.

It is difficult to understand how the leaders of the Protestant noble families could authorise and watch the barbaric scene. Allegiance to the Queen and the new religion came before everything else.

Fortunately, the Deputy Sheriff, George Grenville, was an Oxford man at the same time as Cuthbert, and prevented the worst excesses being carried out, despite the demands from the noble lords. The hanging, drawing and quartering were seen by all before they carried on with their shopping. Even at the end Cuthbert had a chance to save himself if he would specifically implicate Francis Tregian and Sir John Arundell. Again he refused stating, "*I know nothing about them, save they were good and godly gentlemen, and as for the things I am condemned for, they were known only to me and none other.*"

His head was cut off and first hung up on the gate at

Launceston Castle, one quarter of his body was sent to the county town of Bodmin, one to Barnstable where he went to school, one to Tregony near Golden and one to Wadebridge not far from Laherne, the Arundell's home. . Edmund Campion was to hear of Mayne's execution through Gregory Martin and exclaimed, "*We all thank you for your account of Cuthbert's Martyrdom – it gave many of us a real religious joy. Wretch that I am, how has that novice outdistanced me. May he be favourable to his old friend and tutor. I shall boast of these titles now more than ever.*"

As for his death being "*a terror to the Papists*", the opposite was true. Of those arrested only one, Robert Smith, defected and joined the Anglican church. The others, despite loss of lands and imprisonment, held on to the faith. As well as the recusants who had been inspired by his ministry many young men left their remote village homes in Cornwall to go to Douai or Rheims, back to England to martyrdom or exile. As for Richard Grenville thanks, honours and a knighthood were bestowed on him by a grateful Queen for the excellent way he had dealt with "***a matter of religion***".

TREGIAN'S TRIALS

At the time when the priest was going to a quick violent death, his master, the young self-confident squire was languishing in gaol "*closely cabined in Marshalsea*" – in solitary confinement. Having been bound over to remain at Golden, Francis had been summoned before the Privy Council in September 1577. He was charged with entertaining persons of a suspicious character, countenancing superstitious practices and recusancy. The last charge he fully admitted, stating that his refusal to attend the new service was a matter of conscience and implied no ill will to the Queen or Government. The recently knighted Sir Francis Walsingham, the Queen's minister for organizing domestic and foreign spies to seek out the Catholics, interrupted, stating that they must await the outcome of the trial of Cuthbert Mayne which was taking place at Launceston at the same time.

Tregian's importance is seen by the fact that another member of the Council, Thomas Radcliffe, Earl of Sussex, the Lord Chamberlain of the time, invited him to dinner. He tried to get Francis to "behave reasonably". If only he would attend the Anglican Church this "unfortunate fuss" would be over. Francis, as ever, stood his ground and was committed to Marshalsea prison in Southwark. Francis was to remain there until the following June, an important nine months because he came under the direct surveillance of the man who was set to gain his estates if the verdict was guilty, Sir George Carey – who as Knight Marshal was the Governor of Marshalsea. No wonder Francis was kept in solitary confinement.

Some idea of what this meant can be seen today by visiting another Southwark prison, the Clink, which has been kept as a Museum to illustrate the terrible conditions and horrible tortures meted out to prisoners in Elizabethan times. Many Catholics, laymen and priests were to suffer in these two prisons as well as in the Tower. Yet this same area of Bankside was to be the home of a

From this . . .

Golden Manor, Probus, Cornwall

. . . to this

Marshalsea Prison, Southwark, London

protégé of the Knight Marshal, William Shakespeare. Indeed, before Francis was eventually released the Globe theatre was to be built nearby. With its theatres and fairs the area became the centre of "swinging London" where the philosophy of so much of Elizabethan society, "eat, drink and be merry", was enjoyed to the full.

In sharp contrast, Francis was given no opportunity of contact with family or friends, and had barely enough food to keep him alive. There had been no proper trial, no sentence had been passed, though he had been accused at the Launceston trial, in his absence, of receiving an Agnus-Dei and assisting Cuthbert Mayne with the Mass.

In a desperate cry for help he wrote to the Earl of Sussex on October 20. We still have this letter in his own hand. In it he blames Grenville for his troubles, "*some good countryman of mine overlaboured with envy and malice*". Grenville, he felt, had acted against him to cover his own "*foul faults*" of which there were many!

Francis asked to be given a fair trial to proclaim his innocence. He admits there were "*some things by law prohibited found in the custody of my man*" but pleads for his wife and children, stressing Mary's relationship to the Earl and her other noble connections. Despite his loyal ending, "*Your Lordship, whereso it shall please you to use or command him, Francis Tregian*", nothing happened. Sir George Carey saw to that and kept Francis "close cabined" until the following June. Soon after he was informed through the Knight Marshal of the sentence of death passed on Cuthbert Mayne. Francis was again urged to save the priest, and his family, by attending the established church, "*for fashion's sake*".

Francis declared that he "*would not hazard his own soul to hell to withhold Cuthbert's from heaven*". This reply caused the historian, A. L. Rowse, himself a Cornishman, to declare that Francis was "*obviously a self-complacent, fanatic fool of the first water*". Yet, as we have noted, Cuthbert Mayne himself, in his final examination declared that no Catholic should attend the Sacrament, come to church or even hear the new service, "established here in England".

After a number of delays, caused by the fact that some of those arrested at Golden were being tried in Cornwall and some in London, eventually on 9 June 1578 a letter was sent from the Privy Council to the Knight Marshal. It stated that Francis Tregian, "a close prisoner", can be allowed visits from two eminent lawyers, Sir Francis Gawdie, Sergeant-at-law, and Edmund Plowden, a Catholic who was later offered the post of Lord Chancellor if he renounced his religion, but he was to refuse. They were instructed to prepare Tregian for his trial. He was also allowed the visit of a doctor as the rigours of the diet and solitary confinement were taking their toll.

Plowden argued that the indictment under which Tregian was held was "void in law" and asked for the Court's judgement. This was sent back to Carey but he used his powers as Knight Marshal to get the judgement delayed until the assize term ended and the case was dropped. Such was Elizabethan justice! His friends had been brought up from Launceston to join Francis in the trial but now they were all sent back, with Tregian, to appear before the next Assizes in Launceston! Before he left, the Lords of Council asked Francis to recant, thinking that the dreadful imprisonment he had endured would weaken his resolve. Again Francis stood firm. As he was leaving the Council chamber they tried another ploy. He was stopped by a Clerk of the Court, Edmund Tremayne, a fellow Cornishman, who in a friendly way said he was sorry to see Tregian in trouble – perhaps he would like to see "some learned minister" to sort out his doubts about religion. Francis, in the spirit of his very own "learned minister", Cuthbert Mayne, replied that he had no doubts!

A few days later they all set off for Cornwall under the supervision of the new Deputy Sheriff, a former town clerk of Bodmin, who had no love for Francis, and singled him out for specially harsh treatment. He was given the worst horse to ride. Yet Francis was so moved to be out in the fresh air, with the prospect ahead of seeing his wife and family that he "burst into verse".

There is a letter from the Privy Council to the Justices at the Assize in Cornwall urging that Francis Tregian and the others be given a "fair trial" – obviously they had the fiasco of the trial of Cuthbert Mayne in mind. Manwood and Jeffrys were to be the judges again. The jury had four changes, all as malicious as before.

The principal witness for the prosecution was a certain actor, Twigges, who had come to entertain the residents at Golden at Christmas 1575. He declared he had shared a room with Mayne and that Tregian had told him he was a priest from Rome. Francis pointed out that Mayne did not arrive until the following Easter, 1576, and that he could summon forty witnesses to prove that Mayne was at Douai at Christmas 1575. Judge Manwood dismissed this as frivolous! Yet again there was great disagreement between Manwood and Jeffreys. Even the jury tried to get out of making a decision by sending a message to Francis to get him to attend the established church and end the matter. Again Francis refused. He was therefore found guilty of aiding and abetting Cuthbert Mayne in relation to the Papal Bull and in extolling the authority of the Pope, receiving an Agnus-Dei, arranging for Mass to be said, and for refusing to attend church.

GOLDEN IS TAKEN

There were to be yet more delays and suffering for Francis, however. Judge Jeffreys would not accept the verdict, arguing that the Bull was "out of date". Once again the case was referred to a meeting of all the judges. The case against the other prisoners was postponed and they all went back to Launceston gaol for another six months.

Tregian was becoming desperate and managed to get a servant to agree to take letters and money through to friends in London to use their influence in his cause. Again, typically, the plan was thwarted. The servant got no further than Devon before he was arrested. The documents found on him further incriminated Francis.

The Queen's bench of judges refused to pronounce judgement; the stalemate between London and Cornwall seemed never ending. Sir George Carey was now desperate to get his hands on Tregian's land and pushed for a second hearing. At the next Assizes, despite continued support from Jeffreys and Plowden, Judge Manwood won the day. Francis was found guilty on all counts of aiding and abetting Cuthbert Mayne. The penalty was that of praemunire, as expected. Tregian was put outside the protection of the Crown and the law; he forfeited all his lands and his goods, and was to remain in prison for life. It was now 1579, two years since Grenville, now Sir Richard, knocked on his door. Tregian now totally bereft of everything, was thrown into a rat-infested dungeon in the Castle, with twenty abusive and hostile felons, some "three fathoms underground".

Francis was never to see Golden again. Carey was now able to eagerly seize all his lands and goods in the spring of 1579. He arrived at Golden at dead of night, breaking down gates and doors and walls. His men rushed to Mrs Mary Tregian's bedroom and turned her, pregnant as she was, out of doors. Her three young children, Mary aged eight, Francis five, and Adrian just two, suffered the same treatment.

Even authorities in London became alarmed at Sir George Carey's behaviour. He rampaged over half of Cornwall, wherever any acres belonging to Tregian could be found. Some of these lands belonged jointly to Francis and his mother, Mrs Katherine Tregian, and much litigation was to follow. Mary meanwhile had made her way through the fields to the home of some neighbours. She set off for London to contact her influential relatives, especially the Earl of Sussex who had already been trying to help her husband. There was also her brother, Baron John Stourton and her uncle Henry, Earl of Derby. With a man and a maid, Bosgrave, related to Tregian's first cousin, Thomas Bosgrave, another fervent Catholic, Mary set off with borrowed horses saying farewell to Golden forever, on a fine April morning. Only the five-year-old Francis was to return to reclaim the Manor.

On the journey her second daughter, Sibylla, who also has a part to pay in the final stages of the saga, was born. Mary, who was a fine example of those Catholic wives and mothers who supported the recusants in these dark times simply remarked that the new arrival, "*was of some help to poise the panniers and keep them to a better balance*". Mary's faith never wavered. Her support of her husband in over twenty years of imprisonment still to come was always direct, unflinching and immediate.

Fortunately, on arrival in London she was able to stay with her mother, Lady Arundell, in Clerkenwell, where the family had a house. Mary even petitioned the Queen herself but without any apparent result at the time. Francis was still in prison in Launceston during this time consoling himself by writing poetry, and planning an escape overseas.

PRISON POETRY

Eventually Francis was moved to a private room and he was able to express the joy he had on the journey when he wanted to "burst into verse". The problem was that he had nothing to write with! We must therefore judge his poetry in the light of his writing with pin and the snuff of a candle,

> "*For lack of ink, the candle coal,*
> *For pen a pin I use.*"

He doesn't want to be a workman who blames his tools but admits,

> "*They are in truth, more fit to paint*
> *A nettle than a rose.*"

Although Francis does not have the artistic gifts his talented son Francis was later to display, the two poems "*Prayer*" and "*Letter*" show us the soul of the man as he affirms his faith even in the darkest hour of imprisonment. Although he feels he has been treated unjustly by his enemies, yet he prays for them:

> **"As is Thy Holy Ghost O Lord**
> *I pray that Thou would'st spare*
> *The workers of my web of woe,*
> *The causers of my care:*
> *I humbly Thee beseech, O Lord,*
> *Even by Thy blessed Blood,*
> *Forgive their guilt, forgive their ill,*
> *And send them all much good.*"

The other concern in the *Prayer* poem is for himself. He asks that "*foolish fear*" may be expelled and that nothing will separate him from the true Church. Grant, he asks:

"That I never eat profaned
The Lamb without Thy house:
Let not my sins me cause O Lord,
To wander from the Rock,
But grant I may be found in fold
Of Thine afflicted flock."

Tregian's story is an illustration of how this is possible, "*By God's Almighty hand*".

The poem Letter is written to his wife Mary. There are many tender touches but the emphasis is on the way in which prayer will help her and all God's people.

"*Let prayer be your practice, wife,*
Let prayer be your play,
Let prayer be your castle strong,
Let prayer be your fort,
Let prayer be your place of rest,
Let prayer be your port:
Let prayer always plead for grace,
Let prayer purchase right,
Let prayer be your chief delight
By day and eke by night."

With fond farewells to his wife and "my little babes" he ends on a note of hope:

"God send us well to meet again, God send us still relief:
And well to run our restless race, Though rough and full of pain,
That through the blessed Blood of Christ
True glory we may gain."

FAREWELL TO CORNWALL

It is clear from his poetry that Francis was sustained in quite horrendous conditions in Launceston Castle by his personal faith, his hope and vision for the restoration of the Catholic Church in England and by thinking about his enemies in a forgiving spirit. His poetic plea echoes that of the protomartyr of the Church, St Stephen, "*Lord, lay not this sin to their charge*".

Petitions on his behalf were getting nowhere, however, and it seemed to him that the only way to pursue his cause was to escape overseas and work from there. As with all his attempts at subterfuge it went horribly wrong. One of his relatives was convinced that the plan was a good one and boasted that Francis would soon be free! The poor young lad who was set to give the signal was caught, severely tortured and thrown into prison. Yet he never implicated Tregian.

The authorities were now losing patience and Francis was taken out of his private room and put back in the worst dungeon, together with felons. Several attempts were made on his life, on orders from above it is thought. A slow starvation diet of crusts and water was reintroduced, in the hope that it would break his body and spirit.

Suddenly, Mary's petitions on his behalf started to bear fruit. On 14 August 1579 it is recorded that instructions were sent to Mr. Justice Southcote that, "*upon the humble suit of Mistress Tregian, wife of Francis Tregian that he might be removed*". A writ of Habeas Corpus was to be issued moving him from Launceston to the Queen's Bench, Westminster, London. His name is listed in the Annals under "*Papists imprisoned in the King's Bench 1579*". Francis was to enjoy the company of other Catholics here, especially the elderly priests, John Young and Thomas Mirfield. Sadly this support from two men who had lived through these immensely difficult times was taken away. On September 6 Francis was back in solitary confinement because the authorities in Launceston objected to the "*lenient treatment*" Francis was getting. They argued that Mary's petition, based on threats to her husband's life were, "*all lies*".

Once more a change was to come from an unexpected quarter. Sir John Arundell had been arrested yet again. At his trial he denounced Carey before the Council, accusing him of gross injustice in his behaviour in grasping lands which did not belong to him and his involvement in the original arrest of Francis in order to get his lands. As a result of this intervention Francis was allowed to have his wife with him, "*there to remain with him to her liking, but nobody else to come to him; but only on their Lordships special permission*".

There was to be yet another bizarre twist from Cornwall. The officer who had brought Francis up from Launceston now presented his bill for expenses of £50! Francis had no money yet he was threatened that if he did not pay he would be taken back to Launceston at the cost of another £50, thus doubling the debt! The suggestion of Francis that the Queen should pay was not taken seriously! It was left to Mary to gain support from friends and even to sell some of her clothes to raise the £50 so that they could continue to live together as man and wife in London.

The starvation diet and the physical conditions were taking their toll, however. Tregian's health deteriorated rapidly. His family petitioned for alms and for permission to ask for assistance from friends. This was another error as the Council angrily ordered him to be removed from the Queen's Bench to the common gaol of the Fleet in the Ludgate Circus area. He was sent to this notorious prison on 29 August 1580. **He was still there when the new century dawned.**

THE FLEET

As we saw when we looked at Tregian's time in Marshalsea, Southwark, conditions in Elizabethan prisons were very different from those of today. The Warden dealt with all matters in the Fleet prison. This was a highly lucrative post as all the amenities, such as food and bedding, and even the leniency or otherwise of punishments and tortures, had to be paid for!

Those in the Beggars' Ward who paid nothing got nothing but a roof over their head and a stone floor to lie on. Their only "income" would be through holding out a begging bowl through the grate, hoping passers-by would put something in. For the first two years Francis was in the Common Ward, which he shared with a few other recusants but mostly debtors. They all lived and slept in one room. It shows the amazing courage and faith of his wife Mary, that she was came to share these conditions with him and to produce another eight children in prison.

State papers make it clear that Francis was put there "*for disobedience in the causes of religion*". Just as a few years earlier he felt he had to propagate the Faith in Court under the eyes of the Queen now, but a short distance away, he sought to share the faith with the lowest of the low. We have proof of this from an anonymous letter written from a prison inmate to John Alymer, Bishop of London. It notes the comings and goings of Mrs Tregian and describes Francis as the "notablest Papist of all the house", and lists the names of those converted by him. As a result of this letter, signed, "*Nameless because we would be blameless*", his books were taken away and his fellow Catholic, Dr Halsey, who had been helping him in this work, was removed to the Clink. Because of the extremely damp conditions, added to the filth and stench, Francis caught a severe attack of "gaol fever". At the same time Mary was very ill, and gave birth to a stillborn child. The next child, Anne, was to live only a few days. Their stark, sad deaths are recorded in the burial registers of the church of St James, Clerkenwell, the home of Anne's mother, on 15 July 1582 and 25 March 1586.

As a result of his illness, Francis was moved to a single room with fresh air and given a certain amount of freedom "*in the gardens and places of recreation*" which helped him make an amazing recovery. He divided the day into periods of prayer, study and recreation and even learnt foreign languages! Mary was able to live more easily with him, after recovering at her mother's home. It was also possible to have his faithful servant with him, John Phillips, who had been arrested at Golden.

One of his close friends, Nicholas Roscarrock was to share imprisonment with him. He had been arrested at Golden and on release had travelled to Rheims and Rome, returning to his house in London as a member of the Inner Temple. He was caught sheltering the seminary priest St Ralph Sherwin and was in the Tower with him and St Edmund Campion. After those two were martyred he was joined by Sir John Arundell before being moved to the Fleet with Tregian. Of a noble family from St Endellion, near Port Isaac in Cornwall, he wrote much about the saints, especially his own patron saint, and delighted in all matters of history as his "*Register of British Saints*", now in the Cambridge University library, shows. He is thought to be the author of the English *Life of Tregian.*

Unlike Francis, however, on his release he was able to live peacefully to a ripe old age with friends in Norfolk. Information about Nicholas and Francis and the fact that Mary was still able to attend Mass at Clerkenwell, "a very college of wicked Papists", we learn from a planted spy, Benjamin Beard, of the Tichborne family.

CATHOLIC SETBACKS

Because Beard was educated at Winchester and had impressive Catholic connections Francis rather naively took him into his circle of friends. Beard was in prison for debt and therefore was open to bribes from the authorities for his spying activities.

English historians use the spy's evidence to prove that Tregian was an out and out traitor. Yet that very same evidence can be used to show that Francis was totally committed to the Catholic cause both here and in Europe, and through his manservant and Mary kept in close touch with events in the outside world. As the spy remarks, when he was brought bad news, "*he looked wonderfully pale*" and dashed to his room. There were two important setbacks to Catholic restoration at this time. First the beheading of the beautiful and courageous Mary Stuart, Queen of Scots, on 8 February 1587 following Walsingham's discovery of the plot to set her free by her former page, Anthony Babington. During her eighteen years' imprisonment she had served as a symbol of hope for the restoration of the Catholic Faith in England. The other source of hope lay outside the country with Philip II of Spain. The surprising defeat of the Spanish Armada, as much by the winds and the waves as by Drake, was a severe blow.

Government legislation was also making things increasingly difficult. In 1581 the fines for recusancy were increased to £20 for all those over sixteen years of age who refused to attend the parish church. The Arundells are recorded as paying until 1680 – but they were rich and like others used their position to help poorer Catholics and sponsor seminary priests like John Cornelius of Bodmin who went on to preach in the Vatican. The success of the seminary priests in supporting the faithful also brought new severe penalties from the government in the Act of 1585. It declared that any priest found preaching was automatically guilty of high treason. Any person harbouring such a priest was guilty of felony. Penalties of

£100 were levied if any child was sent abroad to places like Douai for education. The anti-Catholic legislation came to its height in 1593 when the term "*Popish Recusants*" was used for the first time, restricting them to certain districts and not allowing them to move more than five miles away from their normal abode.

Actually, to Francis, already confined, this became a privilege rather than a restriction and he was able to move more freely. In 1601 Francis appealed directly to the Queen, asking Sir Robert Cecil to appeal on his behalf. In his letter he claimed the five miles of freedom, promising to come back to the prison every night. He tried to get permission to travel to Bath or Buxton to cure the "*pains of sciatica with which he is continuously and grievously punished*". The Queen seemed favourable at first, but handed the letter to Carey, who of course opposed it calling Tregian an "*agent for the Pope and all traitorous enemies beyond the seas*". Reference was also made to the fact that his son, Francis, was being educated in Rome. The verdict was that he should be sent to Wisbech Castle, in the Cambridgeshire Fens, rather than Bath or Buxton!

This time the Queen overruled Carey, and Francis was given leave to go on parole in Chelsea. Francis immediately took up his countryman's hobby of breeding greyhounds and a year later sent Cecil two puppies for "*her Majesty's clemency*"!

One thing had cheered him up when he was a prisoner in the Fleet, a visit from his son Francis. After a brilliant academic career at Eu, Douai and Rome he had worked for Cardinal Allen delivering his funeral address in Rome in 1594. He was described as being "***very noble, 20 years old, of a happy and natural genius, extremely proficient in philosophy music and the Latin language***". A joy to his father's heart!

INTO EXILE

During the last days in prison help from an unexpected quarter had lifted Tregian's spirits. As ever, this was to be held against him by the authorities then and historians now. The help came from Philip III of Spain, who succeeded his father in 1598. Philip had been taking a friendly interest in Francis for some time, not only sending his personal representative to see him in London but also helping the family with gifts and money. He even made a daily allowance to Francis until this was stopped by Carey, now Lord Hunsdon and Lord Chamberlain, and in possession of Golden.

Accepting money from England's traditional enemy may seem a foolish thing to do but we need to understand the utter deprivation the family suffered. Also, for Francis, Spain remained his only hope for the restoration of the Catholic Church. Had he been free it has been suggested he would have joined the "Spanish party", but his hope went beyond that to a united Catholic Europe with England playing its part again. This is what lay behind his support for the claims of the pious Archduchess Isabella, daughter of Philip II, the Infanta, to follow Elizabeth. Yet even Sir Robert Cecil supported her claims at one stage. Tregian's record and his views meant that on the accession of King James in 1603 he knew it was time to leave. Because of the excellent work done by the seminary priests Catholics were no longer a shepherdless flock and had begun to increase in numbers.

James did not want to "*punish their bodies for the error of their minds*", he just hoped that their bodies would move to the Continent! In one of his first Acts on 19 February 1604, he announced his detestation of the "*superstitious Papist religion*" ordering all Jesuits and priests out of the realm and increasing fines for recusancy. Although neither a Jesuit nor a priest, Francis saw the danger looming and left England in the summer of 1603.

His journey through Europe was like that of a conquering hero, which in a very real sense he was, having conquered his own fears and the anguish of well over twenty years of imprisonment. The Third Douai Diary records how Francis visited the College in July 1603. It notes that he had now given up all hope of regaining his lands, "*long ago seized from him because of the confession of the faith*". His stay at the College was a great consolation both to him and the students and staff there.

In Brussels he saw his son Francis again. The young Francis was now working for Archduke Albert, Regent of the Spanish Netherlands and husband of Isabella, the Infanta.

When Francis arrived in Madrid Philip III arranged a triumphant procession for him through the streets in the Royal Coach. As Francis was about to kneel before the king, Philip raised him up declaring that he was "*honoured to receive one who had suffered so long and lost so much for the Catholic Faith*".

Philip gave him 60 gold pieces a month and, as Portugal now came within his domain, suggested that he should move to Lisbon, with its milder climate for his health's sake.

Tregian, full of surprises to the end, agreed, but asked to live with the Jesuit fathers of St Roque, then on a hill overlooking the city. His final days were spent in prayer and performing good works, passing on the generous donations from the king to the Irish refugees in the city. Gradually his illness confined him to the house. His nurse, Maria Lega, spoke of his joy in those last days, which came, Francis said, from "*a vision of our Lady the Queen of Angels*". His soul had become so full of sweetness that he was able to leave the world without regret. As the burial register there states, "*At sixty years of age our Lord took him to Paradise on 25 September 1608*".

Tregian's last request was to be buried in the church of St Roque, which was granted. The full register entry refers to him as "*An English gentleman, lord of many vassals, but they took from him all his estates*". His body was placed under a flagstone on the right from the entrance by the Chapel of the Holy Sacrament, which was most fitting.

In 1620 this grave was opened up and a body of a young man put on top, and all was reset according to the custom of the time. In 1625 another body was put there.

The flesh of the young man put there five years earlier had entirely disappeared, but the body of Francis, interred seventeen years before, was still there "*incorrupt*" as fresh as it was when buried. A letter written by an English Jesuit, Father Ignatius Stafford from Lisbon on 26 April 1625, to his friend Father Forcer in Madrid, confirms this. Describing what happened the day before on 25 April he refers to Tregian as an "*English Knight*" and remarks that the Fathers gave "***great testimonies of his sanctity***". He goes into rather ghoulish detail about all the parts of the body that remain "*incorrupt*" as well as the Franciscan habit in which the body had been wrapped. The event had been verified by Dom Miguel de Castro, a much respected Archbishop of Lisbon. The streets and the Church and the courtyards were thronged with people of all sorts, day and night, "*especially gentlemen and religious*".

It was then decided to bury him standing up beneath the preacher's chair of the marble pulpit to remind the faithful how he stood up to Elizabeth and all her heresies through the long years of imprisonment. The English Catholics chiselled out the inscription with which we began our story, giving him the honorific title of "Dom" a term used to denote royalty or rank in Portuguese society.

At this time an English College was built in Lisbon for the purpose of training priests to restore the Catholic Faith to England,

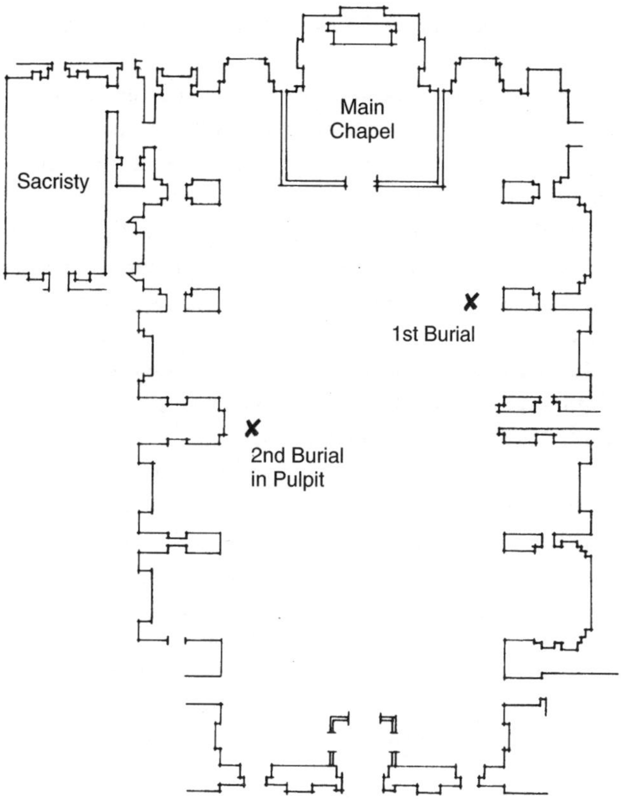

Plan of S. Roque Church, Lisbon

a fitting memorial to the hope which had sustained Francis through the dark years of imprisonment. The first students arrived from Douai in 1628. Francis' grandson, Father Francis Plunkett, was to write of the many miracles linked with Francis and there was a strong move in Lisbon to make him an "unofficial saint". The flagstone under which he was first buried and where the miracle of preservation occurred became a place of great veneration. Flowers and candles were placed there and so many people knelt to pray that the inscription, "*here was found the body of D. Francis Tregian*" was almost worn away.

It appears that the cult got out of hand and the flagstone was removed. Even in the 1950s the biographers Boyan and Lamb could not find it. Thankfully it is now restored, the name still visible but most of the stone worn smooth by the prayers of the faithful inspired by the story of Francis Tregian. Francis Plunkett wrote a poem, ***The Light of the Mirror***, to the "heirs of Francis Tregian". All who find new faith, new hope, new courage through his story are his true heirs.

Unto this mirror's light come turn your eyes.
With Tregian's radiant life the mirror glows
E'en as the mirror holds the sun's bright beam
So Francis from his life shows virtue's ray
The heavenly host all gaze upon this glass
As heaven's own splendour from its brightness grows
If thou wilt also turn thine eyes thereto
Much wealth of piety shalt thou behold
FOR TREGIAN'S VIRTUES STILL RESPLENDENT
SHINE AND IN DEATH'S SILENCE STILL
THEY CRY ALOUD.

The Fitzwilliam Virginal

"Serves as a most important historical document reflecting the musical life of the time"

"Recognised as a treasure house of a most sophisticated keyboard music"

Extracts from the original and
THE FITZWILLIAM VIRGINAL BOOK
by J. A. F. MAITLAND & W. B. SQUIRE, 1899.

published by Brieitkoff & Hartel 1899,

In which they affirm that
FRANCIS TREGIAN JUNIOR
transcribed and arranged the music.

Treg[ian's] Ground.

WILLIAM BYRD.

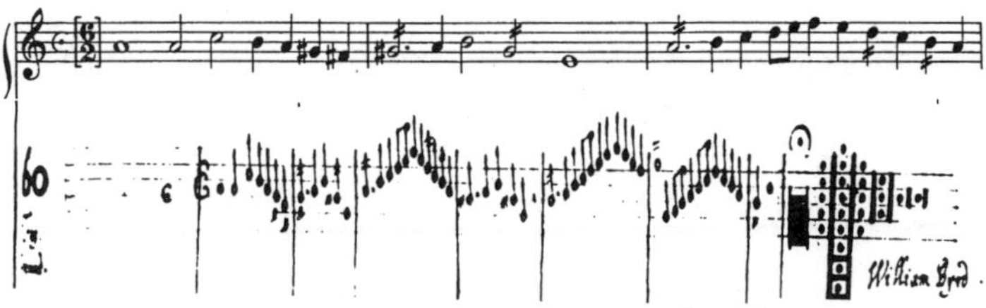

Pauana Doloroso. Treg[ian].

11.

SET BY PETER PHILIPS.

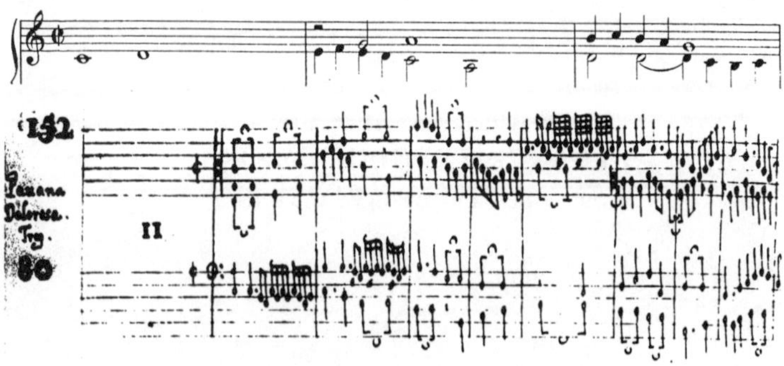

Pavana Chromatica.

Mrs Katherin Tregians Paven.

WILLIAM TISDALL.

TREGIAN'S DESCENDANTS

A recent CD of the music of the Elizabethan composer Peter Philips includes a Ballad **D'Amore** for **Francis Tregian, junior**. The fact that both of them worked at the same time for archduke Albert of the Spanish Netherlands was one of the many clues which have led scholars to confirm that the young Francis was the transcriber of what is now known as the **Fitzwilliam Virginal** now in the Fitzwilliam Museum, Cambridge, containing works of the famous church musician, **William Byrd**.

Again it is the prison spy at the Fleet who gives a direct link between the families when he refers to **Mrs Mary Tregian and her daughter Sybil (Sibylla)** meeting with the **Byrd family**. In the Virginal itself we have Byrd's own work dedicated to the family, "*TREGIAN'S GROUND*". There is also a Pavane dedicated to the young Tregian's grandmother, ***Mrs Katherine Tregian***. A Pavane by Peter Philips has the note "*PAVANA DOLOROSA. TREG(IAN)*". The initials "*S.T.*" could refer to **Sybil**.

Francis junior deserves fuller treatment and we have already noted his story as it was linked with his father. After working in the Netherlands he returned to claim Golden and the estates on the death of his father. Under the law of praemunire they should have been returned to him but he had to buy out the interest in the estates of Lady Hunsdon, widow of Carey. He had to sell the important Manor of Trewithen to pay and the money was handed over in Blackfriars in 1613. His own recusancy and the fact that he had "*borne arms against the friends of Queen Elizabeth*" by working for the Archduke, meant that he followed his father to the Fleet in 1614. It is here that he is known to have been working on a special book for two years. Scholars now agree this must have been the Virginal. At his death his sisters had great difficulty in obtaining the book. He was buried in St Brides Church, Fleet Street on 11 August 1617.

THE TREGIAN PEDIGREE (c. 1450–1650)

Thomas Tregian
(Attorney and Shipowner. In 1456 ship *Mary* licensed to take pilgrims to Santiago de Compostella)

John

Thomas b.1460
(owned ship *Jesus*. Married 1. Elizabeth Penwarne 2. Margaret Borlase)

John b.1490 (d. 15 Apr.1537 m. **1. Jane Wolvedon 2. Susan Crewes**) — Peers — Jane — Thomasine (m.Lanyon) — Sir Reynold (Priest) — Paul — William — Vivien — Thomas (m. Margaret Ashton)

John b.1520 (d. 20 Mar. 1575. m. **Katherine Arundell**) — Elizabeth (m. Sir Richard Edgcumbe) — Jane — William — Lazarus — Edmund — Mary — Martha — Katherine

FRANCIS TREGIAN (**b. 1548 d. 25 Sept. 1608 m.MARY STOURTON**) — JANE (m. Thomas Tonkin) — ELIZABETH — MARY

Mary b. 1571 m. Thomas Yate

FRANCIS b. 1574 d. 11 Aug. 1617

Adrian b. 1577 d. young

Sibylla b. 1579 unmarried

Charles b. 1581 d. 16 Sept. 1629

Philippa b. 1589 m. James Plunkett

- **Fr Francis Plunkett** OSB

Katherine unmarried

Dorothy unmarried

Elizabeth unmarried

daughter no name m. R.Haweis

Children of Mary (m. Thomas Yate):

- **Frances** b. 1597 Poor Clare nun d. 28 Jan.1625
- **Catherine** m. T.Heythorp
- **Mary** m.T.Eston d. 19 Apr.1674
- **Anne** b.1604 Poor Clare nun d. 24 Jan.1667
- **Sister Jane FRANCIS** b. 1605 Islington English Franciscan nun d. 18 Mar.1659 in Belgium

Note: Francis and Mary had two more children in prison: 1).Stillborn d. 15 July 1582; 2).Anne d. after a few days, 25 March 1586, in Clerkenwell. The present TRUDGIAN FAMILY is descended from FRANCIS TREGIAN'S Uncles: WILLIAM, LAZARUS and EDMUND, who were born at GOLDEN.

His brother **Charles**, born in prison in 1581, was also educated overseas at Rheims and Rome. The two were together at **Cardinal Allen**'s funeral there in 1594. He also displayed an exceptional talent for learning, especially in the field of literature. In contrast to his brother he was rather a hothead, composing rude songs about the nobility and followed Francis to the Fleet and burial at St Brides on 16th Sept 1629.

As **Adrian**, born at Golden, had died young and all the other children recorded are girls there is no direct male line. **Sybil, Katherine, Dorothy** and **Elizabeth** were unmarried, one **unnamed daughter** married a **Richard Haweis.** The eldest daughter **Mary**, born at Golden, married **Thomas Yate.** She had five daughters, **Catherine** married Thomas Heythorp and **Mary** married Thomas Eston and the other three became **nuns. Frances** died eight years after professing as a **Poor Clare** at Gravelines at the age of 20 in 1617, described as "*truly zealous of all perfection*". **Anne** also made her profession as a **Poor Clare** at Gravelines when she was 18 in 1621. She died at Rouen at the age of 65 commended for her "*religious comportment, singular sweetness, piety and devotion*". **Jane** joined the order of English Franciscans in Brussels taking the name of **Sister Jane Francis.** She became mistress of the Novices and was given to much prayer and solitude as she patiently coped with a great infirmity, dying in 1659. Her confessor, **Father Francis Bell,** refers to "***the great veneration of the body of her grandfather in the Jesuit Church in Lisbon***" **Philippa married James Plunkett** and moved to Ireland. Their son was the **Francis** who wrote the life of his grandfather in 1655, Lisbon, *HEROUM SPECULUM.* The **Plunketts** of Ireland are the direct descendants and claims have been made by them to recover Golden and they did get a grant from the estates in 1661. The present **Trudgians** "*poor peasants on the land they once owned*" descend through Francis Tregian's father's three brothers, **William, Lazarus and Edmund.**

SOURCES USED

FRANCIS TREGIAN (Cornish Recusant) *P. Boyan and G. Lamb* (Sheed & Ward, 1955).

HISTOIRE d'une famille anglaise: LES TREGIANS. *Helen Trudgian* (Paris 1934).

JOURNAL of the ROYAL INSTITUTION of CORNWALL:—

FRANCIS TREGIAN: His family & possessions *Rev. T. Taylor*, Vol. XVIII, 1910.

The supposed PRIESTS HIDING PLACES, GOLDEN, Probus *H. M. Whitley*, Vol. XIII, 1895.

LOG BOOKS OF GOLDEN MANOR FOR THE PERIOD (*Truro Museum*).

TUDOR CORNWALL *A. L. Rowse* (Jonathan Cape, 1941).

THE PORTUGESE Marion Kaplan (Penguin, 1991).

THE SEMINARY PRIESTS (1. Elizabethan) *Fr Godfrey Anstruther OP* (St. Edmunds, 1968).

FORTY MARTYRS OF ENGLAND & WALES *Fr James Walsh* (Catholic Truth Society).

BLESSED CUTHBERT MAYNE (Westminster Archives) P. Boyan (Catholic Truth Society, 1961).

BLESSED CUTHBERT MAYNE *Frank Davey* (Longman, 1960).

SNOW ON THE HEDGES *Helen Whelan* (Fowler & Wright, 1984).

CARDINAL WILLIAM ALLEN *Stewart Foster OSM* (Catholic Truth Society, 1993).

ST. MARGARET CLITHEROW *Fr John Abrami O. Carm.* (Carmelite Press, 1980).

SAINTS OF CORNWALL *Catherine Rachel John* (Dyllanson Truran, 1981).

Penguin DICTIONARY OF SAINTS (Revised) *C. R. John & D. Attwater* (1995).

Oxford DICTIONARY OF SAINTS (Revised) David Farmer (1996).

A SAINT IN THE FAMILY *S. & E. Usherwood* (St. Pauls, 1992).

CATHOLIC LOYALISM in Elizabethan England *A. Pritchard* (Scolar, 1979).

THE ELIZABETHAN PERSECUTION *A. H. Atteridge* (Harding & More, 1928)

THE HUNTED PRIEST (John Gerard) *Philip Caraman SJ* (Fontana, 1959).

THE GUNPOWDER PLOT *Antonia Fraser* (Weidenfeld & Nicolson, 1996).

SIR RICHARD GRENVILLE *G.H. Bushnell* (Harrap, 1936).

THE LADY MARY (TUDOR) *M. Waldman* (Collins, 1972).

THE ENGLAND OF ELIZABETH *A.L.Rowse* (Macmillan, 1950).

THE REFORMATION *Owen Chadwick* (Pelican History Series, 1964).

THE REFORMATION ERA *H.J. Grimm* (Macmillan, 1958).

CHURCH & PEOPLE 1450–1660 *Claire Cross* (Fontana, 1976).

THE ENGLISH REFORMATION *A.G. Dickens* (Batsford, 1989).

VISITS

ROME – several times, including PAPAL AUDIENCE 1987.

LISBON – Church of S. Roque & Museum. Pilgrimage to FATIMA.

WESTMINSTER CATHEDRAL & The Catholic Truth Society on the Piazza.

CORNWALL – GOLDEN, Probus & Parish Church, Trudgian Farm, St. Ewe, Truro Museum.

SOUTHWARK Cathedral, The Clink Prison & Museum, The Local Studies Library.

The Globe Theatre (Production of Shakespeare's "The Winter's Tale") (MARSHALSEA).

ST. BRIDES Church & Crypt, Fleet Street (Francis Jnr & brother Charles buried here from nearby FLEET prison).

The Lamb & The Flag Catholic Study Centre, Lostwitiel, Cornwall.

The Lamb & The Flag Public House & St. John's College, Oxford.

Fitzwilliam Museum, Cambridge (Study of the Virginal).

St. Margaret Clitherow's House & Shrine, York.

Conversations with Ted Worral, The Recusant Society, Enfield, Middlesex.

Correspondence with Father Pearse Bolster, Ilfracombe, Devon.

Acknowledgements

The author would like to express his thanks to all those who have willingly given permission to reproduce the following documents and illustrations.

To Elisabeth Woollard for permission to use the portrait of Francis Tregian on the front cover and the painting of the Tregyan Coat of Arms on the back cover in memory of her father T. Peter Francis Trudgian, who spent forty years researching the history of his family.

To The Right Reverend Christopher Budd, Bishop of Plymouth, for permission to reproduce the prayer for the Beatification of Francis Tregian.

To Southwark Local Studies Library, London, for permission to use the print of Marshalsea Prison.

Music from the Fitzwilliam Virginal is used by permission of the Fitzwilliam Museum, Cambridge, to whom rights in this publication are assigned.

Front cover: Painting of Francis Tregian.

Back cover: The Armorial Bearings of the family of Tregyan of Wolfedon appearing in colour in a transcript at the College of Arms, of the Herald's Visitation of Devon and Cornwall of 1531.
Arms: Ermine with Three Red Eagles on Sable.
Crest: An Eagle displayed, holding a Sword in its Dexter Claw.

About the author

Raymond Francis Trudgian is a former Head of Religious Studies. He has combined his studies in Tudor Church History at the universities of Cambridge and London, with detailed research in Cornwall and Lisbon to show that his family was at the centre of political and religious controversy in the Elizabethan period.

INDEX

Act of Uniformity (1549), 6
Albert, Archduke, 35, 41
Allen, Cardinal William, 10, 33, 44
Alymer, John, 30
Arundell, Sir John, 5, 15, 17, 29, 31
Arundell, Katherine, 5
Arundell, Lady, 25
Augustine, Saint, 3

Babington, Anthony, 32
Bainbridge, William, 13–14
Beard, Benjamin, 31–2
Bell, Father Francis, 44
Bosgrave (maid), 25
Bosgrave, Thomas, 25
Bourne, Anthony, 14
Boyan, P., 38
Byrd, William, 3, 41

Campion, Edmund, 11, 18, 31
Carey, Sir George, 13, 22, 33, 34
  denounced by Arundell, 29
  Governor of Marshalsea, 19, 21
  seizure of Golden, 24–5
Castro, Dom Miguel de, 36
Cecil, Sir Robert, 33, 34
Cornelius, John, 32
Cranmer, Thomas, 6

Derby, Henry, 5th Earl of, 25
Drake, Sir Francis, 32

Edgcumbe, Sir Richard, 5
Elizabeth I, 3, 7, 13, 33
Eston, Thomas, 44
Evingham, Richard, 11

Fitzwilliam Virginal, 3, 41
Forcer, Father, 36
Ford, Thomas, 11
Francis, Sister Jane, 44

Gawdie, Sir Francis, 22
Golden Manor, 4, 24–5, 41
Gregory I, Pope, 3
Gregory XIII, Pope, 11
Grenville, George, 16, 17
Grenville, Richard, 5, 13, 18, 21
  arrest of Mayne, 14, 15
  Mayne's trial, 16
Grey, Eleanor, 5
Grey, Thomas, 5

Halsey, Dr, 30
Haweis, Richard, 44
Heythorp, Thomas, 44
Hodges, John, 17
Hunsdon, Lady, 41

Isabella, Archduchess, 34

James I, 34
Jeffreys, Sir John, 15, 16, 23, 24
John III, King, 1

Lamb, G., 38
Lega, Maria, 35
Letter poem, 27
The Light of the Mirror, 38

Manwood, Sir Roger, 15, 16, 23, 24
Martin, Gregory, 10–11, 14, 18
Mayne, Cuthbert, 10–12, 13, 19, 21, 23
  martyrdom, 3, 15–18
Mirfield, Thomas, 28

Paine, John, 11
Perne, Dr, 9
Philip II of Spain, 32
Philip III of Spain, 34, 35
Philips, Peter, 41

Phillips, John, 31
Pius V, Pope, 6, 7
Plowden, Edward, 22, 24
Plunkett, Father Francis, 7, 37, 38, 44
Plunkett, James, 44
Popham, Sir John, 15
Prayer poem, 26–7

Radcliffe, Thomas, Earl of Sussex, 19, 21, 25
Regnans in Excelsis, 7
Roscarrock, Nicholas, 15, 31
Rowse, A.L., 21

St. Roque church, 1, 36–7
Shakespeare, William, 21
Sherwin, Ralph, 31
Smith, Robert, 18
Southcote, Justice, 28
Stafford, Father Ignatius, 36
Stephen, Saint, 28
Stourton, Baron John, 25
Stuart, Mary, 32

Tregian, Adrian, 24, 44
Tregian, Anne, 30–1
Tregian, Charles, 44
Tregian, Dorothy, 44
Tregian, Edmund, 44
Tregian, Elizabeth (aunt), 5

Tregian, Elizabeth (daughter), 44
Tregian, Francis (1548–1608), 1–3, 5
  arrest and trials, 15, 19–23
  burial, 36
  Catholic Faith, 3, 6–7, 9
  death, 35
  Fleet prison, 29–32
  Launceston Castle prison, 24, 28–9
  leaves England (1603), 34–5
  Marshalsea prison, 19–21
  poetry, 26–7
  Queen's Bench imprisonment, 28–9
  second hearing judgement (1579), 24
Tregian, Francis (son) (1574–1617), 3, 24, 25, 26, 33, 35, 41–4
Tregian, John, 4
Tregian, John (1490–1537), 4–5, 6
Tregian, John (1520–1575), 5
Tregian, Katherine (daughter), 44
Tregian, Katherine (mother), 25, 41
Tregian, Lazarus, 44
Tregian, Mary (daughter), 24, 44
Tregian, Mary (wife), 5, 21, 29
  Byrd family, 41
  Fleet prison, 30, 31
  forced from Golden, 24, 25
  petitions, 28
Tregian, Philippa, 44
Tregian, Sibylla, 25, 41, 44
Tregian, Thomas (junior), 4
Tregian, Thomas (senior), 4
Tregian, William, 44
Tremayne, Edmund, 22
Trewarthenick, Joanne, 4
Trewarthenick, Stephen, 4
Twigges (actor), 23

Walsingham, Sir Francis, 19, 32
Wolveden, Jane, 4

Xavier, Saint Francis, 1

Yate, Anne, 44
Yate, Catherine, 44
Yate, Frances, 44
Yate, Jane, 44
Yate, Mary, 44
Yate, Thomas, 44
Young, John, 28